One Shall Chase a Thousand

Book 9 of the Junior Jaffray Collection of Missionary Stories

Written by Barbara Hibschman

Illustrated by Elynne Chudnovsky
Cover Design by Step One Design
Portrait by Karl Foster
Based on *One Shall Chase a Thousand* by Mabel Francis

CHRISTIAN PUBLICATIONS / Camp Hill, Pennsylvania

 **The mark of vibrant faith**

Christian Publications
Publishing House of The Christian
and Missionary Alliance
3825 Hartzdale Drive, Camp Hill, PA 17011

© 1993 by Christian Publications
All rights reserved
ISBN: 0-87509-516-X
Printed in the United States of America

93 94 95 96 97 5 4 3 2 1

Unless otherwise indicated, Scripture taken from the HOLY BIBLE: NEW INTERNATIONAL VERSION. Copyright © 1973, 1978, 1984 by the International Bible Society. Used by permission of Zondervan Bible Publishers.

Chapter 1

Mabel's New Heart

"Mabel and Gertrude, please come here," called Father. The two sisters headed toward the kitchen.

"Now, girls, you are big enough to help Mother in the kitchen. Gertrude, I want you to wash the dishes. Mabel, you can dry them."

"Okay, Father," agreed Gertrude. "It'll be fun to help in the kitchen."

Mabel stared out the window. She didn't say a word.

Father noticed her frowning face and asked, "What's wrong, Mabel?"

"I don't want to work. I want to play. I hate drying dishes. Anyway, I feel sick today."

Before Father could say any more, Mabel ran out of the room to her favorite hiding place. *No one will find me in the closet*, she thought. *They'll never look behind Father's big winter coat.*

Mabel pulled the door shut. It was very dark in the closet. She could hear Father and Mother calling her. When she thought the dishes were done, she peeked out the closet door.

Mother was putting the last plate in the cupboard. Mabel felt ashamed of herself. She should have helped with the dishes.

The longer Mabel stayed in the closet the worse she felt. She finally realized she had to come out, even if it meant being punished.

"I'm sorry I made a fuss," Mabel cried. "I promise I'll help tomorrow."

When Mabel's family finished their breakfast the next morning she started to help with the dishes. All of a sudden she remembered how she hated to dry dishes.

"My head hurts," she began to whine. "Please let me go lie down for a little while." Again Mabel had fooled everyone.

The next morning after breakfast, Mabel went to the kitchen sink. She looked at the pan full of dirty dishes. *There are so many of them,* she thought. *This is going to take a long time. I hate drying dishes.*

Mabel kept thinking of how much she didn't want to help. She would rather go outside and play.

"Oh, Gertrude," Mabel yelled, "I think I'm going to throw up!" Mabel held her stomach and ran out of the kitchen screaming like she was really hurt.

You would think Mabel would have been a happy person because she got her own way, but she wasn't. The more she pretended to be sick, the more she had to tell lies. And the more she lied, the worse she felt. She knew disobeying her parents and telling lies were wrong. She knew she was selfish and naughty.

One night, Mabel felt so bad she got down on her knees and prayed, "Dear Jesus, I'm sorry for being so selfish and wanting my own way all the time. Please forgive me and come into my heart. Help me not to complain and make a fuss. Help me to please You and my parents."

The next day after breakfast Mabel followed Gertrude into the kitchen. She started to help carry the dishes to the sink and then that same feeling came back—she didn't want to do dishes.

But this time Mabel prayed instead of complaining.

"Dear Jesus, I still don't like to do dishes, but I want to try to please You. Please help me not to make a fuss."

Mabel went right on working. She didn't pretend to be sick and she didn't complain. In no time at all the dishes were washed, dried and put away.

  One day Father said, "Why, Mabel, you're such a good helper." That made Mabel very happy. She knew God had answered her prayer. He had taken her selfish heart and given her a new loving heart that wanted to help others.

Chapter 2

Mabel Goes to Camp

"Giddy-up, Nick," shouted Father so the old horse would trot a little faster.

"He must be tired," said Mabel. "I know I am. Yesterday wasn't so bad, but today it seems like it's taking forever to get to camp."

Mabel's father made a cracking noise with the leather strap on the harness. Father was tired, too.

"We're almost there," he said. "It shouldn't be long now."

As Mabel rode in the carriage beside her father she felt like butterflies were floating around in her stomach. She was excited to go to Old Orchard Camp. She would see friends from last summer and maybe some from the year before.

Mabel had some news to tell them. During the year, God had spoken to her heart and she was going to be a missionary to Japan someday.

Someday seems so far away, thought Mabel. *Before I can go to*

Japan I will have to go to college and that takes a lot of money. I wonder how long it will take me to save up enough money?

"I see the tents and cottages now!" announced one of the other children from the back of the carriage.

"Me, too!" shouted Mabel's sister, Anne.

The summer breeze was nice and cool as it blew through the tall pine trees. She stretched her neck until she could see the benches lined up on the grass like church pews underneath the clear blue sky.

Hundreds of people came to Old Orchard to hear a very famous man preach. His name was Dr. Albert Simpson. Dr. Simpson loved God and wanted to send missionaries around the world so everyone could hear about Jesus, the Savior.

Mabel especially liked it when the offering was taken.

One time some of the women took off their jewelry and put it in the offering basket. When one lady had given all of her money and all of her jewelry she shouted, "If the offering basket were larger, I would get in myself!" She wanted God to have everything she had.

Sometimes people who were crippled and sick asked Dr. Simpson to pray for them. Many were healed.

The last day of camp Dr. Simpson showed some pictures of the Nyack Missionary Training Institute in New York. Mabel thought it would be the right place for her to go to college before she went to Japan. But there was just one problem—she didn't have enough money.

After the meeting, a woman named Mrs. Rose came up to her and asked, "Are you planning on going to the Missionary Training Institute?"

"I want to go," answered Mabel, "but I don't have the money to go to school now."

Mrs. Rose smiled.

"I've been watching you. I think you need to be in school at Nyack," she said. "If you decide to go, I will pay your school bill."

"Oh my, that would be wonderful!" said Mabel.

She thought her heart was going to burst with joy. She ran to her family back at the cottage.

"It's a miracle," she cried. "God just did something special for me. I know He will always take care of me—even in Japan."

Chapter 3

"Kon-ni-chi-wa"

Have you ever been on a really long trip? Maybe, not long after you left home, you asked your Mommy or Daddy, "Are we there yet?"

Mabel Francis went on a *very* long trip. Her trip was to Japan on a big boat. Day after day the ship rocked back and forth, back and forth, back and forth.

Finally, after many days, it docked in Japan and Mabel was so glad to be on land again. She had been seasick almost the whole time.

"Hello, my name is Mabel Francis," she said to a Japanese woman standing near the dock. The woman looked at her, but didn't speak. Do you know why? The lady couldn't understand or speak English! And, of course, Mabel couldn't speak Japanese!

I must begin learning the Japanese language so I can make some friends, thought Mabel.

The Japanese language is very hard to learn because it doesn't use letters like A, B, C. Japanese letters

are called characters and there are thousands of them.

Would you like to see what some of the characters look like? Turn to page 22. Look at the church sign. It says, "Matsuyama Community Christian Church." How would you like to have to learn to write Japanese?

A young girl came to Mabel's house every day to help her learn Japanese. Mabel practiced the words over and over again. Finally, she was able to greet the people she met on the street by saying "Good-day." In Japanese it sounded like this, *Kon-ni-chi-wa*. Can you say, *Kon-ni-chi-wa*?

Another problem Mabel had when she arrived in Japan was finding a way to travel. There were no cars or buses and the trains were very slow. Most of the people went from place to place in rickshaws. A rickshaw is a cart that is pulled by a man. That was too slow for Mabel, too.

So Mabel had an idea. *I'll get a bicycle*, she thought to herself. *Then I can really go places and meet some new friends.*

Mabel loved riding her bicycle up and down and around the mountains and along the streets and trails.

One day she saw a Japanese family eating supper. The fish, rice and vegetables smelled so good as she passed by on her bike. She noticed that they didn't eat with a spoon or fork or knife. Instead, they used chopsticks.

They weren't sitting on chairs either. They sat on straw mats on the floor beside a little table with short legs.

Another day Mabel saw a Japanese mother and her two children walking in a beautiful garden.

"Clip-clop, clip-clop, clip-clop," sounded their wooden sandals on the bridge.

"Kon-ni-chi-wa," greeted Mabel.

"Kon-ni-chi-wa," answered the children. The mother smiled shyly at Mabel. Maybe she was a little bit afraid because Mabel didn't look anything like the Japanese people. Her checkered dress from America was nothing like the *kimonos* that the Japanese wore.

The *kimonos* looked strange to Mabel, too. She giggled to herself, *They look like bathrobes. But they look very comfortable, too.* Mabel learned to enjoy wearing *kimonos*.

One day Mabel was visiting in a

Japanese house. She noticed that this home, like most Japanese homes, had a special shelf with flowers, food, pictures of relatives, or idols on it. Every day the people prayed to these pictures or carved statues made out of wood, stone or gold.

They prayed to idols because they didn't know anything about the one, true God and Jesus who is the only One who can take their sins away.

Mabel felt sad when she saw the people praying to idols. She knew that those idols could not hear any prayers.

"Dear Father," she prayed, "how can one little person like me tell all the people of Japan about You and Your love for them?"

Mabel decided that she would make a whole lot of friends. So day after day as she rode her bicycle and met new people she would say, *"Kon-ni-chi-wa."* She invited them to her house for tea.

It wasn't long until Mabel had some friends who wanted to know more about the true God who was not on a shelf.

Chapter 4

Fearless Mabel

Mabel lived in the city of Matsuyama. Her sister, Anne, was also a missionary in Japan and together they taught women and children about Jesus—until one day an awful thing happened. The war!

Japan and the United States were fighting each other. Many missionaries left Japan to come home to America. Mabel and Anne wondered if they should leave, too.

"I can't imagine leaving Japan," Mabel told Anne.

But Anne was worried.

"If we stay, what will happen to us?" she wanted to know.

Anne remembered hearing about other wars. People got hurt in wars and many died.

"I don't know," whispered Mabel, "but I do know God's love for the Japanese people doesn't change just because there is a war. I came here because God sent me here. I must stay!"

Anne was not so sure about staying, but she finally agreed.

"We can't leave now," added

Mabel. "We can't leave because we're afraid of what might happen. God promises us in the Bible that He is with us. He said, 'Do not fear, for I am with you'. He will take care of us, Anne. We must trust Him."

The war was awful. Many bad things happened. Many people were hurt and many died. Homes, schools, churches and other buildings burned or fell to the ground because of the bombs. People didn't have places to stay out of the rain, wind and cold. Many people starved to death because there wasn't enough food.

But Mabel and Anne had a place to stay! They were Americans and Americans were now the enemies of the Japanese. So Mabel and Anne were put in prison.

Mabel's prison was a large house where other women prisoners were kept. She could not leave the house and no one could come to visit her. She missed her Japanese friends, but most of all she missed her sister. Anne had been put in a different prison.

On many lonely days and nights Mabel reminded herself of God's promise. She knew He was with her because the Bible said so. She prayed that Anne would know that God was with her, too.

Many long days went by and there really wasn't enough food. The women prisoners were given only one piece of bread in the morning and one in the evening. Mabel was so hungry she couldn't go to sleep at night. And when it was time to get up in the morning, she was even more hungry.

One morning, a policeman told the women, "There will be no bread today. There isn't any flour. You can't make bread without flour."

But Mabel remembered God's promise: "Do not fear, for I am with you." She knew God would take care of her even if there wasn't any bread.

Later that day, the policeman came back to the house with a Japanese lady. She had some fresh spinach from her garden. The prisoners hadn't tasted fresh vegetables for a long time. They were so thankful to have something to eat—even spinach.

As Mabel ate the spinach she knew in her heart that God was keeping His promise. She didn't need to worry or be afraid. He was taking care of her today. And He would take care of her tomorrow.

Chapter 5

Good Things Happen at Church

Mabel and Anne were so happy when the war finally ended. As soon as they could they went back to Matsuyama where they used to live. They wanted to see how all their friends were. They wanted to see if the church building was still standing after the bombs and fires.

When they got off the train in Matsuyama they were shocked. The city looked like one big garbage pile. They didn't know which way to go. They walked and walked until they came to what they thought was their old neighborhood.

All they could see at first was the metal frames of trucks that had been burned and piles of trash that had once been buildings. Mabel's house was gone. Anne's house was gone. And the church building was gone.

As she wiped the tears from her eyes, Mabel said, "We must build the church again. So many good things happen at church. The people need a place to worship God and learn how to follow Him."

"It's impossible, Mabel," said Anne as she shook her head. "What can we do? There is no wood or nails or lumber around to build a church. And there are no stores, so we can't buy anything."

"But there is something we can do," suggested Mabel. "We can pray and ask God what to do. I know He wants a church here in Matsuyama. He'll help us to know what to do."

So Anne and Mabel prayed, asking God to show them how they could get some materials to start building a church.

One day Mabel and Anne heard some people talking. The news was that some American soldiers were going to leave Japan now that the war was over.

"Did you hear that, Mabel?" whispered Anne. "They're going to abandon the Army base."

"Yes, I heard it," answered Mabel. "If it's true, there will be lots of materials there that they won't take back to America. Even the things they throw away will be valuable to us. Let's go visit the commander and see what we can find out."

The next day Mabel and Anne went to the Army base. They knocked on the officer's door. A big man with kind blue eyes greeted them. He was surprised to see two American ladies knocking on his door.

"Where did you come from?" he smiled. "Please come in."

Mabel and Anne told the officer all about their work at the church in Matsuyama before the war. They told him the church had been destroyed. They asked him if there might be some materials on the base the Army didn't want.

"We would be glad to have even a board," Mabel told him.

The officer thought for a few moments.

"There is a house that has to be torn down," he finally said. "You can have anything you want."

Mabel and Anne were as excited as two little girls in a doll shop. There were lots of things—wires, boards, sheets of iron, a table and many other things they could use.

"We'll take it all," announced Mabel.

"That's fine, ladies," said the officer, smiling to himself. "I'm glad you can use it. There's only one problem—you must have it off the base in three days."

Three days? Mabel wondered how two little ladies could tear down a house and haul all the materials away in just three days. But she did know that God must have a plan.

"Yes, sir," Mabel answered. "Thank you for your help. I don't know how we'll get it all done. We don't even have a hammer, but I know it will all work out."

"Oh, that's not a problem," said the officer. "We have hammers you can borrow."

Mabel and Anne got the hammers and started to tear down the house. A Japanese boy, walking by, noticed the two American ladies pulling nails from some boards. He offered to help.

They worked and worked, loosening nails and pulling apart boards and sheets of iron. They piled them on the ground so they could load them on a truck.

"A truck? Where are we going to find a truck? How are we going to carry all of these things into the city?" asked Anne.

"I don't know. It seems impossible! But God knows we can't do it alone," replied Mabel.

Can you guess what Anne and Mabel did? They did what they

had done before when things looked impossible. They prayed. They asked God what to do.

"Dear Father," they prayed, "You know all about our problem. Please help us to find a way to get all of this stuff into the city."

As the sun was going down and it was almost dark, a big American Army truck stopped right where Mabel, Anne and the Japanese boy were working.

"We're here to help you!" the driver called out the window.

"You are?" smiled Mabel. "Who told you we were here?"

"The officer was worried about you," the driver explained. "He didn't know how you could move all of the materials into the city, so he sent me to help you."

Soon all the materials were loaded into the truck. What an exciting day they had had!

Good things began to happen after the Matsuyama Community Church was built. People from all over the city came to the church to hear God's Word and learn about His great love for them.

As Mabel had said earlier, "So many good things happen at church."

Chapter 6

Mabel Is a Champion

Do you know what a champion is?

A champion is someone who does something very well.

Maybe you know the name of a famous football player who you think might be a champion?

Or perhaps you've watched ice skaters on TV when one was chosen to receive a gold medal because she skated well.

Or maybe your sister got all 100's on her spelling tests every week last year in school. She could be called a champion speller because she spells very well.

Well, Mabel Francis was a champion, too. No, she wasn't a champion football player or skater or speller, but she did something very well.

One day, when Mabel was very old, she received a special invitation. It was from the Emperor of Japan. Mabel was invited to appear before Japan's highest government leaders. Can you imagine how excited you would feel if you were asked to go to the White House to appear before the President of the United States?

Mabel's heart pounded with excitement. There were lots of people gathered in the room. The Japanese official opened a beautiful scroll that had the Emperor's seal on it.

He read out loud the list of things Mabel was being honored for. It was a list of all the ways she had helped the Japanese people after the war.

The official presented her with a gold medal and made her a member of the Fifth Order of Sacred Treasure. That also made her a citizen of Japan, even though she was an American.

It was a very special honor because Mabel was the only person who had ever received the medal while they were still alive. No one else had been honored like that.

What was it Mabel Francis did very well? What made her a champion?

She loved and obeyed God enough to go to Japan and stay with her Japanese people during the war. She loved the Japanese people.

She helped the ones that were hurting. She took care of the sick. She took food and clothing to those that needed it. She visited people who were in prison like she had been. She taught them about the true God. They saw what Jesus was like by watching how she loved others more than herself.

She also helped build churches where people could meet together to pray, sing and learn God's Word. She even started a kindergarten were Japanese boys and girls could hear Bible stories, sing happy songs, make things and play together.

Yes, Mabel Francis was a champion because she did something very well—she loved God and she lived to help other people.

God can help you be a champion, too.

THE JUNIOR JAFFRAY
COLLECTION OF MISSIONARY STORIES

For additional copies of *One Shall Chase a Thousand* or information about other titles in the **Junior Jaffray Collection of Missionary Stories**, contact your local Christian bookstore or call Christian Publications toll-free at 1-800-233-4443.

*Titles coincide with the adult biography series, **The Jaffray Collection of Missionary Portraits**.